RETURNING LIGHT

For Steve —
with gratitude for
your work + words,
+ the joy of participating with you
in "authors Night"
at the Wieli Library !
4/13/10

Lisa
Sowberg

ALSO BY LISA SORNBERGER

Stone and Feather (chapbook)

RETURNING LIGHT

Poems by

Lisa Sornberger

Antrim House

Simsbury, Connecticut

Library of Congress Control Number: 2008939169

ISBN 978-0-9817883-1-9

Printed & bound by United Graphics, Inc.

First Edition, 2008

Book Design: Rennie McQuilkin
Photograph of Author: John Sornberger
Cover Painting ("Moongirl"): Sandy Mastroni

Antrim House
860.217.0023
AntrimHouse@comcast.net
www.AntrimHouseBooks.com
P.O. Box 111, Tariffville, CT 06081

ACKNOWLEDGMENTS

Some of the poems in this collection appeared in a chapbook entitled *Stone and Feather,* and some were first published, often in earlier versions, by the following journals, whose editors I wish to thank:

Common Ground Review: "Cumberland Island"
Fairfield Review: "Wild Ponies at Chincoteague"
Ginosko Literary Review: "Winter Bones"
New Virginia Review: "Eggplant"
Take Two: They're Small (anthology): "Eggplant"

I also wish to thank the Stadler Center for Poetry, Bucknell University, for the gift of a fellowship, and the Wesleyan Writers Conference, for that of a scholarship.

Gratitude to Jill Robinson, Morgan Lance, and all at Animals Asia Foundation for their humane work in helping Moon Bears and other animals in Asia.

Deepest thanks to Rennie McQuilkin, whose vision and generosity have helped to bring this book into being, and to Sandy Mastroni, my friend whose painting graces the cover. It has been my pleasure to work with you both on this project.

I am grateful to teachers, friends, and family for their support, and would like to acknowledge Hugh Blumenfeld, Carol Chasse, Swami Sahajananda, Ilona Sakalauskas, John Sornberger, and Alexander Taylor for their specific contributions.

Thank you to my mother and father for your gifts of love and language.

for John, my love

TABLE OF CONTENTS

Meditate.
Live purely. Be quiet.
Do your work with mastery.
Like the moon, come out
from behind the clouds!
Shine.

attributed to The Buddha

You've got to shake your fists at lightning now
You've got to roar like forest fire
You've got to spread your light like blazes
All across the sky.

from "Judgement of the Moon and Stars," Joni Mitchell

RETURNING
LIGHT

Catch Fire

MEDITATION

Night blossoms —
petals brilliant blue,
a gentian.

Imagine a hand
palm up, fingers opening,
giving us everything.

LILIES

Jesus said to consider the lilies, and I do.
And although he meant lilies of the field,
I conjure lotuses afloat on a lake,

stars drifting on dark,
tethered by tendrils,
roots grown tangled,

fixed in thick muck,
yet the flowers they birth
transcend earth,

balance on water,
breathe in tune with moon and sun.
They open according to light.

Night-Blooming Cereus

The plant I'd had for years,
scraggly and awkward,
strange-leafed and mottled,
grew its first bud this summer

and began to blossom today:
its flower head bent,
trembled, lifted, and fell
ever so slightly, and this evening

it quickened its pace
outside the glass door
of the place where I sat with friends
at the hour chosen weeks before

to light a candle, burn incense and sage
in meditation and prayer for our teacher,
gone on ahead.
We finished, opened our eyes,

observed it push itself open
into a waxy white star,
a pulsar from light years away
whose perfume permeated the sky

for a single night. It called
sphinx moths to visit

the sweet vanilla nectar
in the second star

at its heart
and beckoned us
to absorb its fragrance,
witness its natural miracle.

The Meteorologist in her Garden

The roses ramble at odd angles to sun;
I have never attempted to count them.

There are hybrids, prize-winners,
and something wild I will never tame.

It is my favorite, there, in the corner,
barely contained, that gorgeous red

with the headiest scent
in its unmade bed.

This is where the work of logic falls apart,
with its predictions and calculations,

where joy comes together.
I am reminded of the way

a waterfall tumbles as if at random,
though the freefall is reasonable as gravity,

yet out of the reaches of constraint.
There is that much pleasure here.

I find comfort in the chaos
as I do nowhere else —

everything blooms and changes
with or without my forecast.

EGGPLANT

You grow out of a flower,
slip into your own skin,
purple as midnight's silk horizon,
the way that sunset
transforms itself into night.
You are the way
land embraces light,
the perfect curve of melding
heaven and earth,
union of spirit and skin.
Suspended from a tenuous stem,
you touch and taste the earth,
reminding us that our birthright
is to delight, to shine,
to be unafraid of being flesh.
You are as purple as acted-on passion,
heady as grapes ripened to full readiness,
Eve's gift in September's garden.

TRAVELER AT WATCH HILL

I'm home again,
walk the beach to Napatree Point,
plant my feet
in shifting sand.

I want to outrun old sun,
outshine full moon tide.
Waves erase my walk
easily as the magic slate pictures
I made as a child.

Still I belong to this place
same as starfish and sandpiper,
artemesia and sand rose,
all that lives and dies and grows.
Sea oats and silica sand,
wind-polished,
shine.

CUMBERLAND ISLAND

After winter's storms, barrier islands
replenish themselves from deep sea.

In spring, I return to Cumberland
where dark gives itself to light,
sand marries sea.

I move into my center,
jump into my own wild heart, that river.

Swim into my fin, wing, bone.
All that lives pulls hard toward home.

WHITE HORSES

"The sight of wild white horses is a vision of angels."
                    –Edward Frank Allen, *The Complete Dream Book*

They emerge from fog
like clouds separating themselves
from sky, shaping into something else —

wild white horses
that enter the field, hoof and sniff
the rain-sweetened air. Distance

comes closer. I know them by heart,
have ridden them through dark,
held on to their necks,

then watched them pull away,
lifting into the air,
their shoulder muscles working like wings.

I have felt their freedom,
felt myself falling,
feeling my way toward the earth.

ANIMAL GUIDES

I hear them calling:
I leave my home and people,
wander deep into night forest.

I burn sage,
stare into fire, wait.
They come to me.

Wildcat roars in my belly,
dark horse bucks and whinnies,
bird flies out of my throat.

Each brings her wisdom,
guides me through dark.
I belong here now.

The wildcat gives me fierceness,
the dark horse, freedom,
the bird, bittersweet song.

All tell me the path to home
runs through my belly, heart, and head.
I am willing at last to be led.

CAVE WOMAN

My body.
Primeval place.
I am here.
Moss hair,
root feet,
cave.
In my center,
in my belly,
my animals live.
I go down,
follow my breath,
bring light to dark.
There's a wild horse painted on the wall.
Rat and slug and salamander crawl
and slither in mud,
and sound rises from perpetual river.
I reach into the water,
touch ghost fish that swim sightless.
I hold a lotus
that opens and closes
according to light.
It is my heart.

ANATOMY CLASS

Massage students learn bone by touch.
How to landmark
by *process* and *fossa.*

We handle the weight of bones,
hold them apart,
weigh them against one another,

try to know them with eyes closed,
envision them under each other's skin
lit up as in an x-ray.

We speak in scientific terms
while we learn the invisible language
of touch, made palpable and real

by Kirlian photography,
galvanic skin response,
electromagnetic fields that radiate

like our talk, lifting us up
into other realms,
none of them far apart.

We see chakras mapped on our bodies
like stars, with their low pulsing hum
always calling us,

their vibrational song
the endless *om*...
that brings us back to our bones.

The Heart

That Mystery

Postcard from the Country of my Dreams

Forget Italy.
Pisa's leaning,
Venice is sinking.
Come to me!
The weather is better here.
We'll romp on the beach,
swim naked,
drink pink champagne,
eat jackfruit and kumquat.
Forget the Sistine Chapel stars.
We'll make the fiery midnight sky ours.
We'll sleep beneath the Southern Cross,
make love a prayer that guides the lost.
Forget Italy.
Come to me!

FOR JOHN

I gather you in my hungry hands
that want everything,

memorize the lines in your face
with my finger,

press breasts and belly into you
as you enter me, and I you.

We confirm our recognition
by sign of our secret stars, birthmarks

left and right of breastbone
where we match where we meet,

spirit to spirit.
They guide us home, each to each.

NAMES

I could be *Cloud Feather,*
Light Conjurer,

Word Dancer,
She Who Wards Off The Dark.

You could be *He With His Child's Heart,*
Man With The Ocean Eyes,

Ground Walker,
Shining Pool of Still Water —

We could be happy there.

At the Feast of St. Joseph

The women lay down their gifts
by the feet of Jesus,

baskets of handmade bread
shaped into bones and other body parts.

These are tangible prayers
for the sick and the suffering.

I would offer up a wishing bone
and lay down my love at your feet.

323 MASS. AVE.

The open roses in your window make me wonder —
I could knock upon your door,
explain my heart —
how light touched it,
slant light that fell upon your flowers
while flowers fell,
petal by petal
onto the windowsill
into the falling sun.

I could tell you how a stranger's house seemed familiar.

I could tell you that I loved you.

Just something about those roses.
And the passing of the season.

PICASSO'S GIFT

You show up at the garden gate,
no flowers in your hands,

no Pinot Noir, no bakery cake,
no cherry pie that you didn't make.

You bring your wildness to my door,
your windy hair, your fire,

your painting of a troubled sea,
your warm eyes burning right through me.

I thought the things I loved were wrong.
I longed for what I thought I lacked.

You help me discover my way
each time you come to bring me back.

You bring your wildness to my door,
your windy hair, your stars,

your hands that tilt my face to yours
and hold me plain in morning light.

FOR SARA, AT FIFTY

for Sara Elizabeth Schermerhorn Hinman

Girlfriend, here's to happiness, that hat trick.
Age has its fine points: like scotch, we mellow.

Half centenarian and half Barbie,
so tell me, is the moon half full or half empty?

Ah, here's to the heartaches that forced our hearts open,
prescriptions that kept us half stoned, half sane;

to breaking and crying,
comfort and healing

and falling through childhood
and digging through dreams.

To the gifts that are found
in sifting through rubble.

Here's to laughter, and the humor
of those who have sorrowed,

and to traveling, traveling,
traveling light.

WILD PONIES AT CHINCOTEAGUE

The sun lays down its body
where light falls from sky.

Today, a painter walked this beach,
almost alone,
filling his pocket with stone and feather,
bits of bone and polished sea glass.

He gathered light on canvas.
He'd come to paint the wild ponies,
manes and tails, shining and easy,
the brush flying freely!

Their hearts are their mystery.
Wild ponies pounding down the beach,
their hoofbeats like
his heartbeat against my body.

His heart is still a mystery to me.
He shapeshifts, lifts into flight,
disappears down the beach—
out of sight, out of reach.

Wild geese ahead of their cries
leave me below to witness and listen.

Narcissus

Love's ghost rises in the hall of mirrors.
I am a mirror there, hung upon your wall,

empty of all but your image.
Reflections of yourself keep you company.

I sing, but you cannot hear me:
I am merely your sound gatherer,

listener to one who hears only his echo.
It is the curse you carry alone into evening.

Hearing everything, that is my cross.
This is your world, I'm just a prop in the scenery.

You are everywhere,
everywhere.

Winter Bones

Winter is black and white in farmers' fields.
Balance in opposites, cool comfort in geometry.
Stark stubble in parallel rows

was once corn and wheat,
planted perpendicular,
each to each.

Now there's just cow and crow,
ground holding up sky,
fence folding into field,

the way a rib cage
guards, yet exposes,
a heart.

Today seemed like a dream, and it was.
You and I reached for one another,
released each other.

Parting is itself a gift:
you break my heart
wide open.

Your flesh is still more vivid than my own.
But I am returning.

Tonight I sit beside a fire,

knit a sweater
to hold and warm my winter bones.
Stone and feather.

Stone of Sadness

Lightness of Flight

POET

"You've got the disease, you might as well get the diagnosis"
                                                                                        -J.C.S.

How strange the good days,
your frame hunched over a table,

your fingers flying on keys
trying to ride the wave of words

that tumbles out of your mind,
trying to balance itself on the page...

Oh you've never been normal
(I might as well say it!) —

prone to passions, to mood swings, to mania,
drawn to pulsing word magic,

stomach knotted in joy at the library,
your cherished collection of words on scrap paper...

word devotion, word obsession,
always trying to find the perfect word!

You dream in detail in iambic pentameter,
the Muses sing to you deep in your sleep,

you wake talking to their voices in your head —
"Only speak the word and I shall be healed."

JACK-IN-THE-BOX

Wacked-out, insomniac,
Jack paces back and forth,
forth and back.

Alive between dreams
and strung too tight,
he closes the window
to hold back the night.
Writing is a reason
to leave on the light.
He types and paces,
paces and types.

The moon is no anchor
in that sea-black sky —
she flies.

Then the sun subtracts Jack,
leaves him faceless, anonymous,
in a panic,
same as he always is —

manic, manic,
temporary.

Clutter

You clutter your house with pretend,
pretend that you'll live long enough

to use all the useless gadgets,
display all the pointless knickknacks,

clean out the basement and empty the closets,
wear all of the outmoded clothes

and dance in your snakeskin boots,
maybe a lampshade on your head —

find a way to make everything passé and tattered
come together and finally make sense.

SCAR POEM

How will I ever come together?
Living proof of union,
I am also evidence of division.

Torn down the middle,
there are places in me
that refuse to smoothly meet,

the ragged edges of a scar.
Forty years later, the past
is ancient history.

I am still trying to pull the opposites toward center.
I am trying to hold the world together.
I am trying to hold light and dark.

IT's EASIER TO LOVE THE DEAD

It's easier to love the dead.
They require little
and ask for less.

Think of all you've loved the best,
with perfect ease,
in retrospect...

FOR LINDA

Your passing is a grief
that startles the heart. How fragile
we all are.

We never knew
your silent patience
or trials of flesh,

sinew twisted, body of bone
grown wrong, tangle of roses in a thicket
by the retaining wall.

Our hands never knew
that they would feel your absence
as palpably as your presence.

Now your image shifts into a shadow
like those burned into sidewalks,
witness to existence and disappearance.

In August

Perseids shimmer, fall from grace
like Luna moths into the blaze;
we give our essence to the night —
our singular bodies burn, turn
into light, brief as a star's trail.

AT A CEMETERY

Birds flirt, they dart
from stone to stone,
perch to worm.

This place is alive.
The day shines,
it lights up the dark

granite and obsidian
where the dead rest
their weary heads forever.

And I am here with them,
touch stone in lieu of flesh,
trace the names of those

my hands long to hold
like light that slips
past the edge of the sky,

no longer lost souls
like the rest of us. We go on
while the Archangel waits,

his beautiful face tipped back,
eyes lifted to heaven
as if wondering when.

SEPTEMBER COMES SOON

Everything changed in a moment.
Or is it that I've just awakened?

I was content in summer slumber,
a cat stretched out in a sun patch.

Now I see the season curling in
on itself, crisp lace edging leaves.

Someone made a fire last night;
the acrid air had a bite to it.

I felt understood by the weather,
old melancholy and me.

MOON BEAR

for Moon Bears everywhere, in captivity and free

You live in the part of our heart
that we are afraid to enter,

in the chamber where suffering dwells,
and awareness of suffering

locked in all of us,
the genuine heart of sadness, as Pema says.

We cannot forever avoid this place
any more than you can your small cage,

where you live awake
in an endless nightmare of pain.

You eat your flesh in frustration,
no hope of escape.

We are our hearts;
to live apart from them is to lie.

To turn away is to lie.
We can honor the sorrow in your eyes.

We are all kin, all mammal.

Beautiful animal, even your name

Moon Bear is lofty, a prayer
for the innocent and suffering everywhere.

SISTERS

I think of you in your kitchen,
as I am preparing the evening meal,

this daily ritual that sisters share
everywhere, regardless of distance.

I imagine you, sipping wine with refinement
from a thin-lipped crystal glass, lovely yet

sharp enough to pierce a heart open
when it's broken.

But in this moment, you hold steady
a light bouquet of Chardonnay;

light shimmers into liquid,
a glimmer from the sun fading

outside your kitchen window,
and a twilight breeze passes through mine.

A coyote's cry rises from the woods
behind someone's home nested in the suburbs.

The moon floats alone above it all,
silent witness to the sun's disappearance.

Everything comes undone.
What's gone is gone, and maybe forever.

CONFESSIONAL POEM

Priest and penitent
inches apart,
bodies so close,
alone in the dark.

THE OTHER

She alters into another,
becomes her mother and father,

loses landmarks — family and friends
now distant cliffs she sails past.

She keeps her heart buried down deep
for ballast, a stone in her chest —

it sinks her, while it steadies her,
guides her over the endless sea.

OF THE BODY

Pain is part of the landscape here,
to be neither avoided nor feared
but navigated and negotiated with.

Living in the body
is like riding in a nameless boat
on a starless night, on a dark river.

If you ask the wind to guide you,
trust the water to hold you
and are willing to talk to trees,

understand animal cries and songs,
and answer them with your own,
you are halfway home.

TRANSMIGRATION

in memory of Harriet McGraw Sornberger

Magic happened in your garden:
plants transformed
into birds and butterflies.

Their blossoms became wings.
Delphinium elatum, "Bluebird"
and *Delphinium grandiflorum,* "Blue Butterfly"

turned into flying things, as dazzling as
Sialia sialis, Papilio Ulysses.
They, like you, transcended themselves,

let go of everything,
even the garden,
to learn how to fly.

GRIEF

I carry the dead too long;
they are gone
their own way now.

They go on,
leave me here,
in my own life,

changed in so many ways
that it is hard some days
to recognize myself,

the mirrors shattered,
shards of glass everywhere.
Still, I *am* —

these eyes to witness,
this voice,
this burning gift.

SNOW ANGELS

for Susan Tyrol Bagcal

We visit after thirty years,
remind each other of who we once were,
our connection weathered, but never lost.

You are familiar as my own face —
you mirror me back
as I was in the old days.

We speak the same language,
a language of possible angels.
But the sky has fallen.

When you tell me your visions
of angels, how I want to believe them,
but none of them comes to me now.

I remember another lifetime,
unbroken by grief.
I remember a day spent as angels,

our backs pressed flat against the cold,
arms sweeping snow that gathered and feathered
and fell from our wings,

and grinning into the north wind,

our talk bold against growing up
and turning old, forgetting everything,

even our promises to stay the same.
Now we have come full circle,
back to the bitter heart of winter,

our backs up against the cold.
You bring me your warmth,
conjure your visions,

hope to convince us both
to give up the weight of our gravity.
Oh how I would love to,

to take on the lightness of flight,
to transcend the stone of my sadness,
rolling that cave door back.

A Memory

in memory of Mary Frances and John Donnelli

My grandparents sat together on the front seat,
and I was in back, steering and singing to myself,

chewing Juicy Fruit gum from the endless stash
in Grandma's deep and generous pocketbook,

home to quarters and curlers and broken things —
like chalk and string and stocking garters.

A Sunday drive after supper — sheer happiness.
The St. Christopher medal on the dash to protect us,

we were off to the *Pocchio Place,* as I called it,
meaning *popsicle,* aka Homestead Dairy.

I was thinking Root Beer Brown
and I was dreaming Sky Blue Pink.

I was smiling out the window
like my bobble-head puppy.

And here and now, forty-five years later,
I'm older than they were then.

Now I see their skin in mine,

thinning ever so slightly,

recognize his gait in my limp
on days when weather fluxes and changes.

I see her ankles in my ankles,
beginning to thicken and slumping

like stockings bagging, but
I still live in this good bag of bones,

this body of hungers,
this body of light.

RESOLUTIONS

Less coffee
more champagne

more singing
less talking

more balance
less black and white

less crying
more dancing

start smoking
give up peppermints

more Mary
less Rhoda

more Marilyn
less Madonna

more reign-it-in cowgirl
fewer apologies

fewer obligations
more collages

less listening
more listening

more showing up
less running

more acknowledging resentment
less resentment

less heartache
more love

more self
more love

more touching darkness
more leaning into light.

SUNDAY MORNING

I talk to our cats,
listen to Bach,

drink Java,
think of God.

Not God of the fear
and the fire,

not God of the penance
nor God of the promise,

but God of the star,
the sheep, and the flower.

God of the open heart,
of the light

and of the dark,
its counterpart.

AT TWILIGHT

There is nothing to say.
Nothing to take away
the ache of the empty place.

The full moon floats,
her ghost body hovers
above the roses of sunset.

The old oaks watch and wait:
wise women who point
thin fingers at the sky.

I wait here, caught between
sky and earth and water,
listen to the sounds

of Canada Geese,
one mourning dove,
and a kingfisher

high in a willow tree
who sings his lonesome song
for someone not me.

Hummingbirds and flycatchers
rustle the rushes, cattails, and reeds
reversed on the surface of this circle

of pond. It mirrors the moon,
moves it below me.
Water striders break the surface,

send its stillness
reverberating into circles,
circles whose paths cross

and overlap, until who knows
where which motion started.
Remembering what's lost,

useless or gone,
now I lose everything,
come into now,

this image of trees
grown deep
and upside down.

I enter this vision,
dive in,

gliding past surfaces
through ice water,
distance,

roots,
rocks,
straight into
and clear through
the bottom of grief.

I fly to the highest branches.

Nothing stops me.

MEDITATION II

Every day we sit with intent
to still the monkey mind
to open the heart,
that ear,
that flower.

We have come here
to listen to God
to lose the illusion of ourselves.

Who will dare to stare straight into the sun
until they go blind, or mad,
until they catch fire?

About the Author

Lisa Sornberger decided to be a writer at the age of nine and weathered adolescence with the aid of the Muse. In her early twenties she met her future husband, John, also a writer, with whom she continues to share joy, much fun, and many adventures, which include house-building and restoration, far-flung traveling, snorkeling, gardening and beach-roaming. She has had an abiding interest in animal protection, its most apparent manifestation being the family of five cats with whom she and John cohabit. For many years and in many capacities, she has helped the disabled; she has also been a licensed massage therapist. Through all of her activities, poetry has been a constant. She is a member of the Thread City Poets and has received several honors for her writing, among them a fellowship to the Bucknell Seminar for Younger Poets, a scholarship to the Wesleyan Writers Conference, and selection to tour with the Connecticut Poetry Circuit's student contingent. Lisa Sornberger's work has appeared in literary journals such as the *New York Quarterly,* the *New Virginia Review, Fairfield Review, Embers,* and *Common Ground Review.* In 2004 her chapbook *Stone and Feather* was published.

To order additional copies of *Returning Light*
or other Antrim House titles, contact the publisher at

Antrim House
P.O. Box 111, Tariffville, CT 06081
860.217.0023, AntrimHouse@comcast.net
or the house website (www.AntrimHouseBooks.com).

•

On the house website
are sample poems, upcoming events,
and a "seminar room" featuring discussion topics
& writing suggestions offered by Antrim House authors
as well as supplemental biography, notes, images and poems.